The Little Book of Character Strengths

June Rousso, Ph.D.

Copyright © 2016 by June Rousso All rights reserved
This book, or parts thereof may not be reproduced in any form without permission from the publisher except for brief excerpts used for reviews.

ISBN 10: 1-937985-62-8
ISBN 13: 978-1-937985-62-2

Printed in the U.S.A.

june.rousso23@gmail.com
www.junerousso.com

The 24 character strengths in this poem are the VIA Classification of Character Strengths. For more information on the VIA character strengths visit: www.viacharacter.org VIA Classification ©Copyright 2004-2018, VIA Institute on Character. All Rights Reserved. Used with Permission.

The Little Book of Character Strengths

Character strengths can be guiding stars in our lives. The VIA Institute on Character researched twenty-four universal strengths that most of us have, some stronger than others but always with room for growth. Once we become aware of our strengths we can learn how to use them effectively and develop them further. The first step is to have a clear understanding of the meaning of each of the strengths. They are presented here as a poem, and for a child and young adult audience.

DEDICATION

Dedicated to my husband, Ira, and his signature character strengths of love of learning, honesty, love, kindness, and humor.

WISDOM

Creativity is shaping your thoughts into something that you have never seen or heard before.

It is letting your imagination go and start to soar.

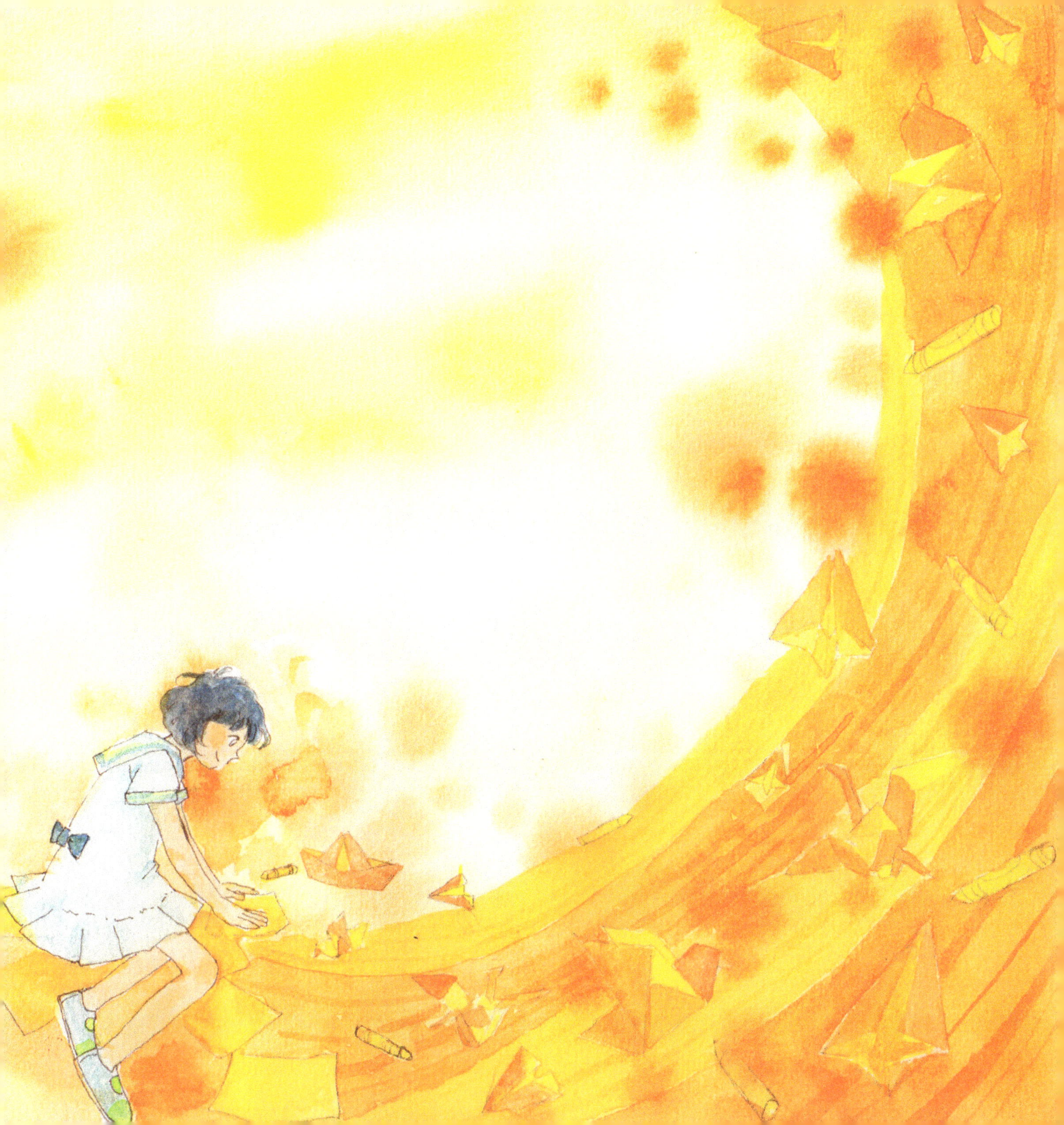

Curiosity is having an open mind and wanting to experience something new every day.

Asking questions to learn more than you do
And in this way bring the world closer to you.

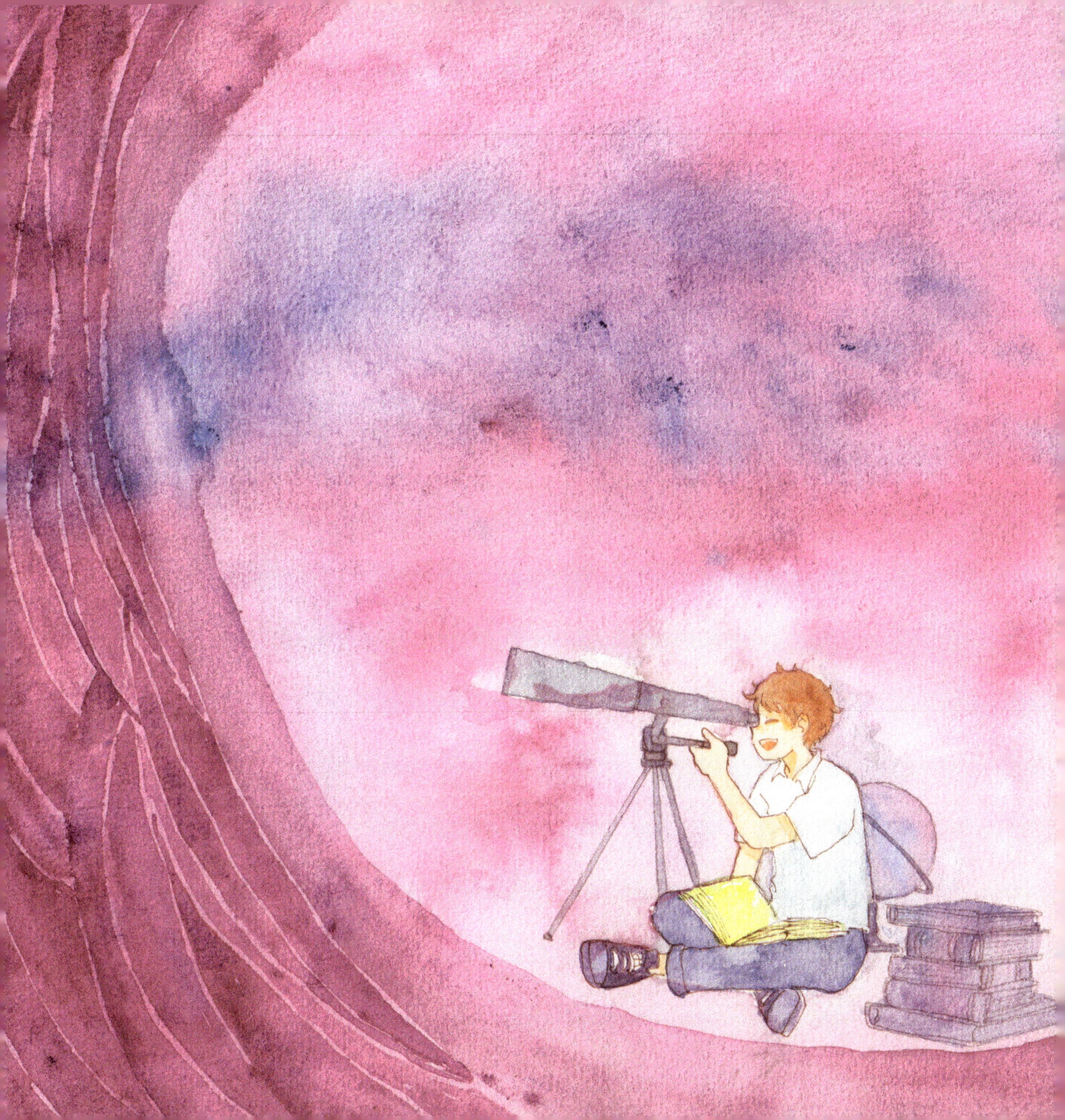

Judgment is thinking things through
Never rushing in what you set out to do.

Changing your mind when new facts come your way
And truly listening to what others have to say.

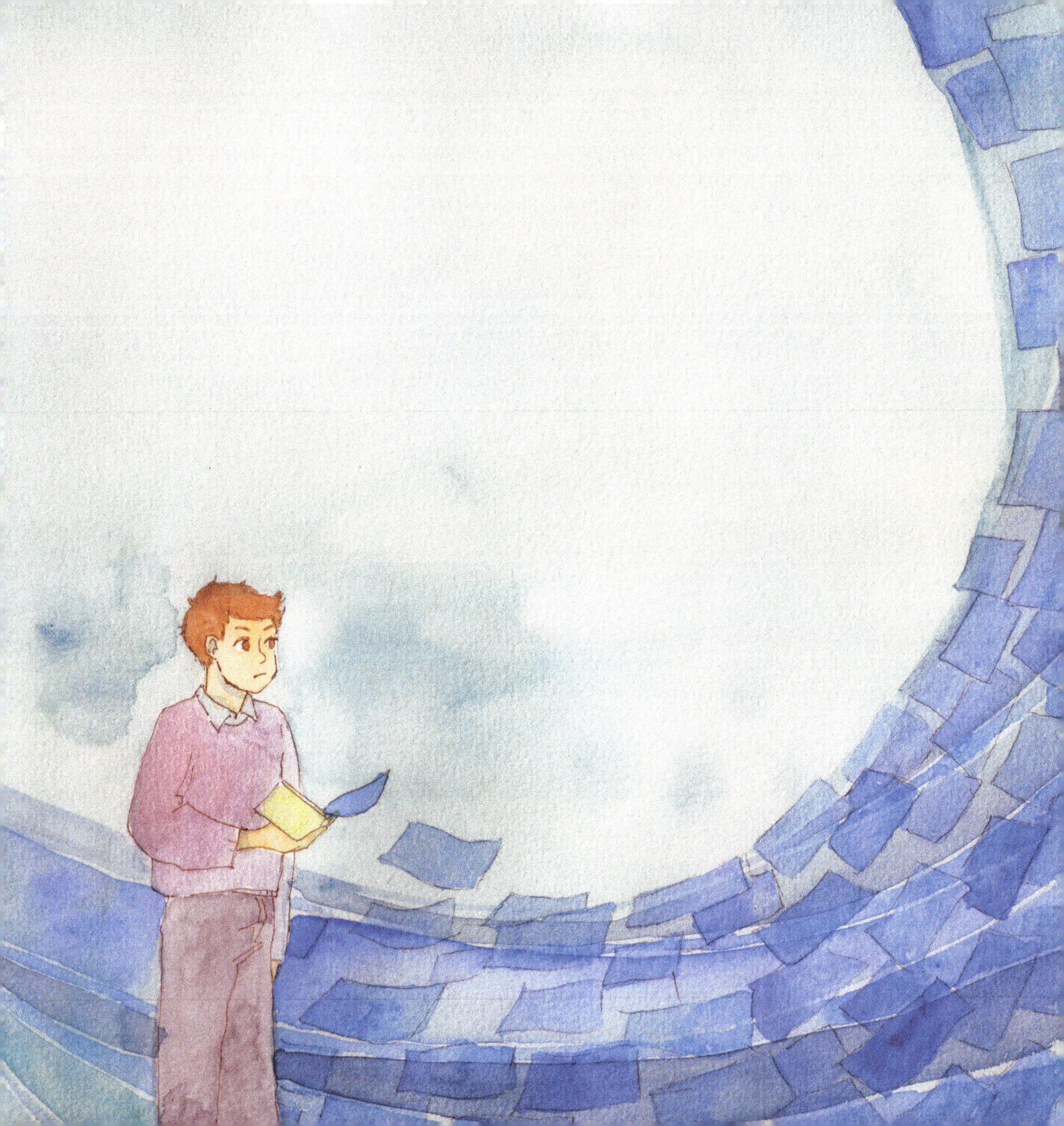

Love of Learning is mastering skills and being in the know.
Learning something new wherever you go.

Some from what you read and others from the people you meet.
Always learning - what a treat!

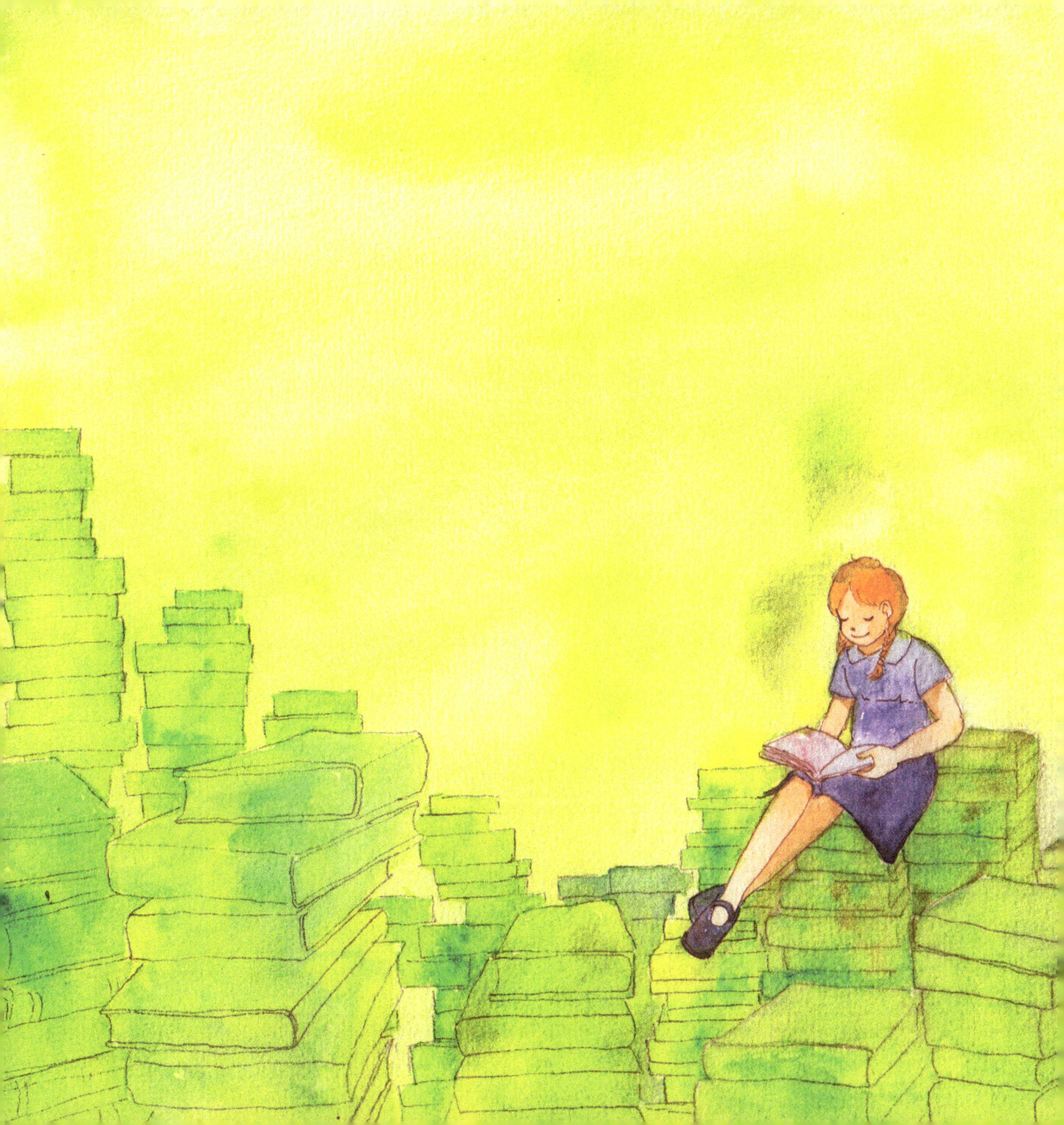

Perspective is using your intelligence and common sense
in deciding what to do.

It's not being foolish, but taking time to
think things through.

Learning not to always ask others for advice.
Believing that our own good judgment can suffice.

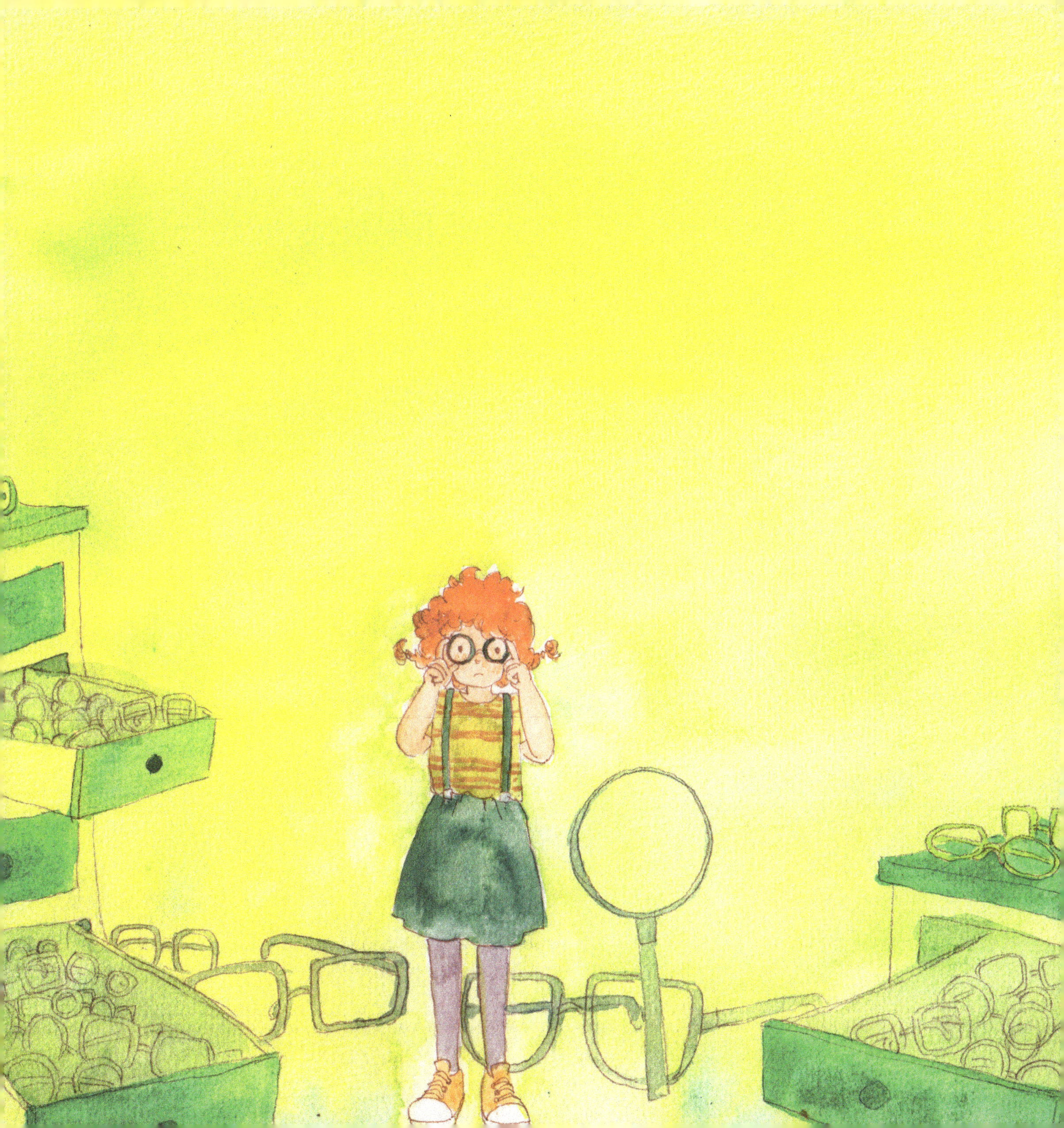

COURAGE

Bravery is trying new things and taking risks
Even when you feel afraid and may start to shake.

It's moving forward
Without thinking much about making a mistake.

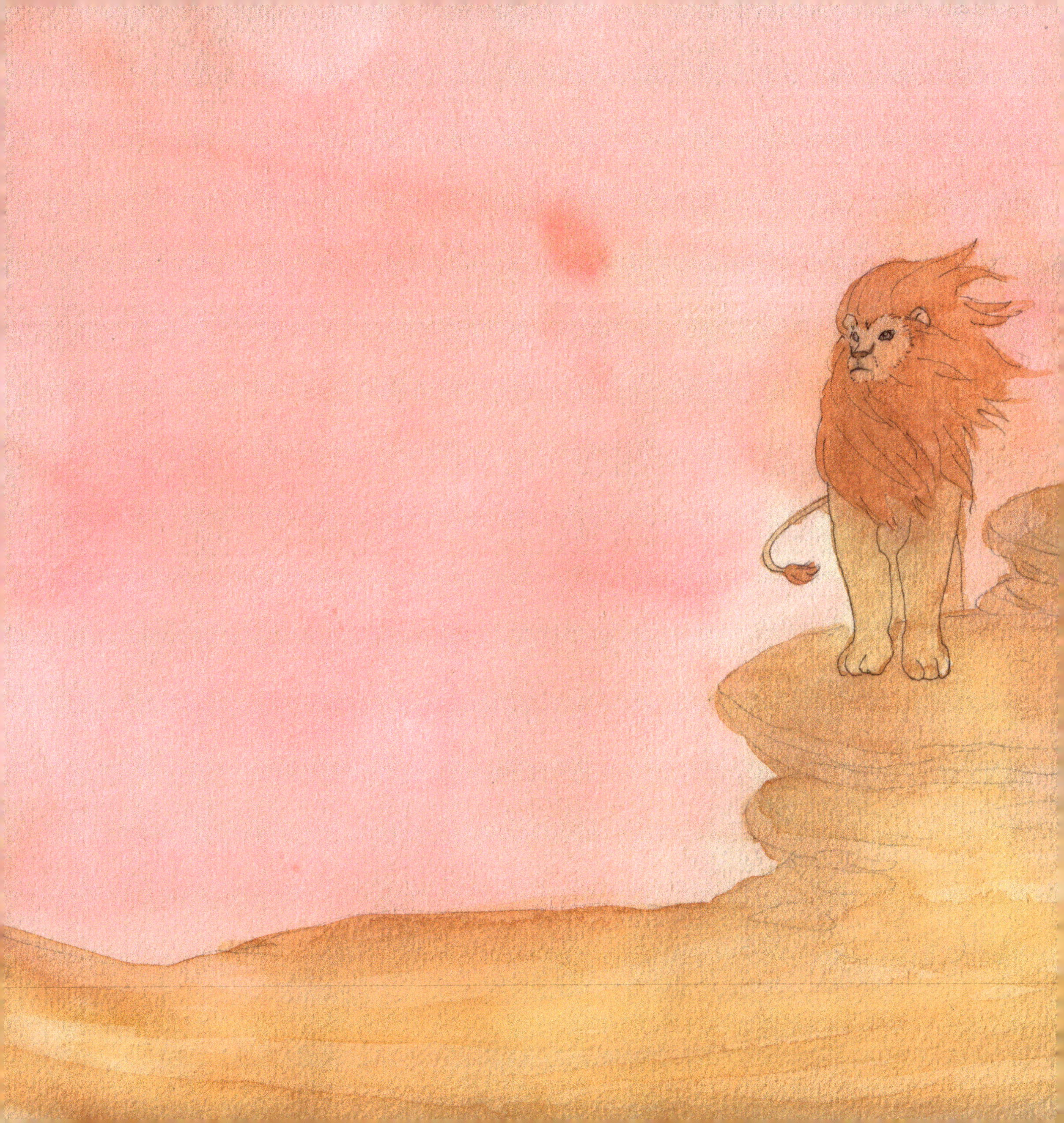

Perseverance is working hard to complete what we start
And not getting so upset that we fall apart.

It's taking things step-by-step, that's for sure.
In this way, we can always achieve more.

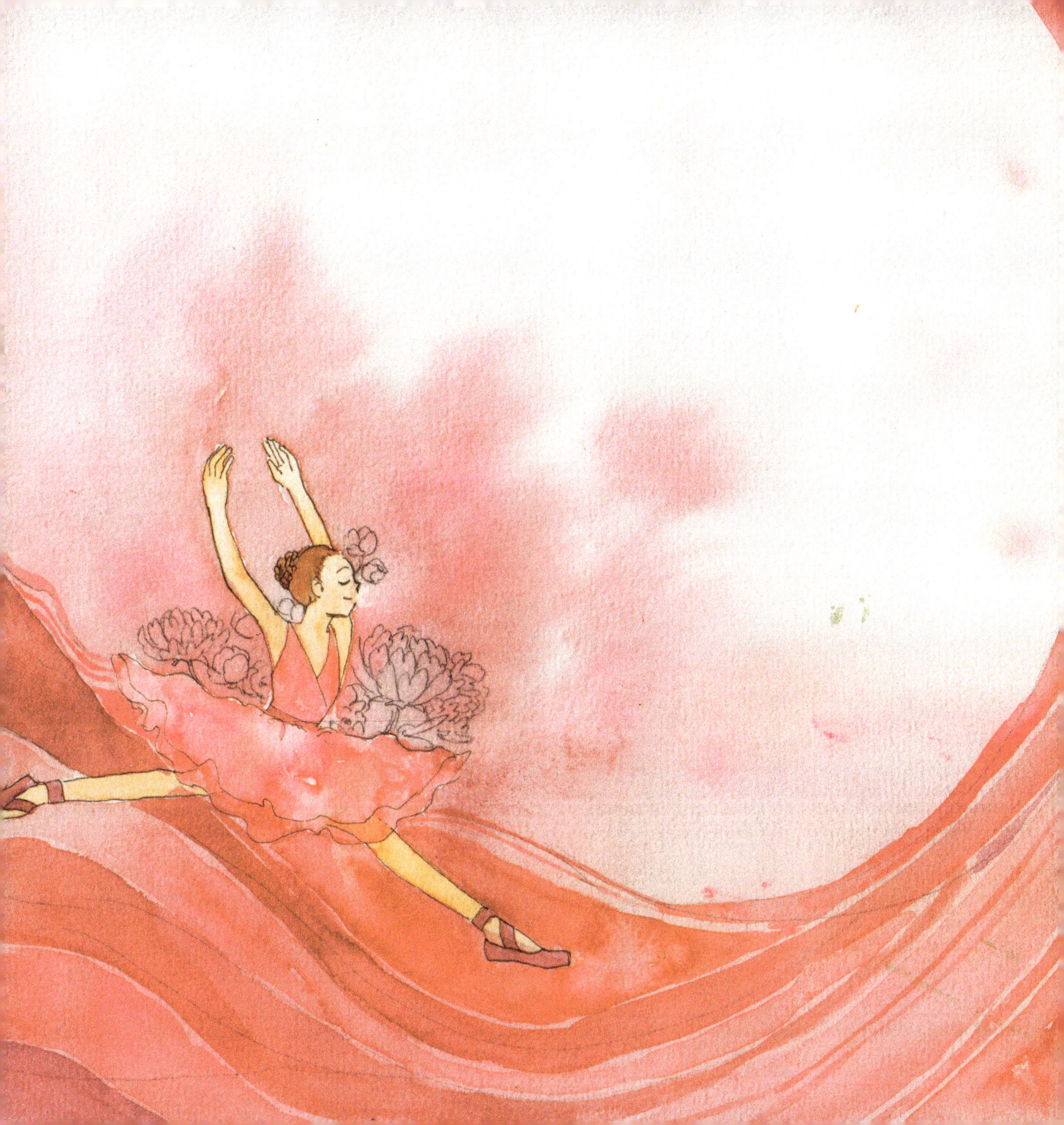

Honesty is being true to ourselves.
Taking responsibility for our actions and not looking to blame,
Not trying to give anyone a bad name.
Nor looking at fibbing and telling tales as just a fun game.

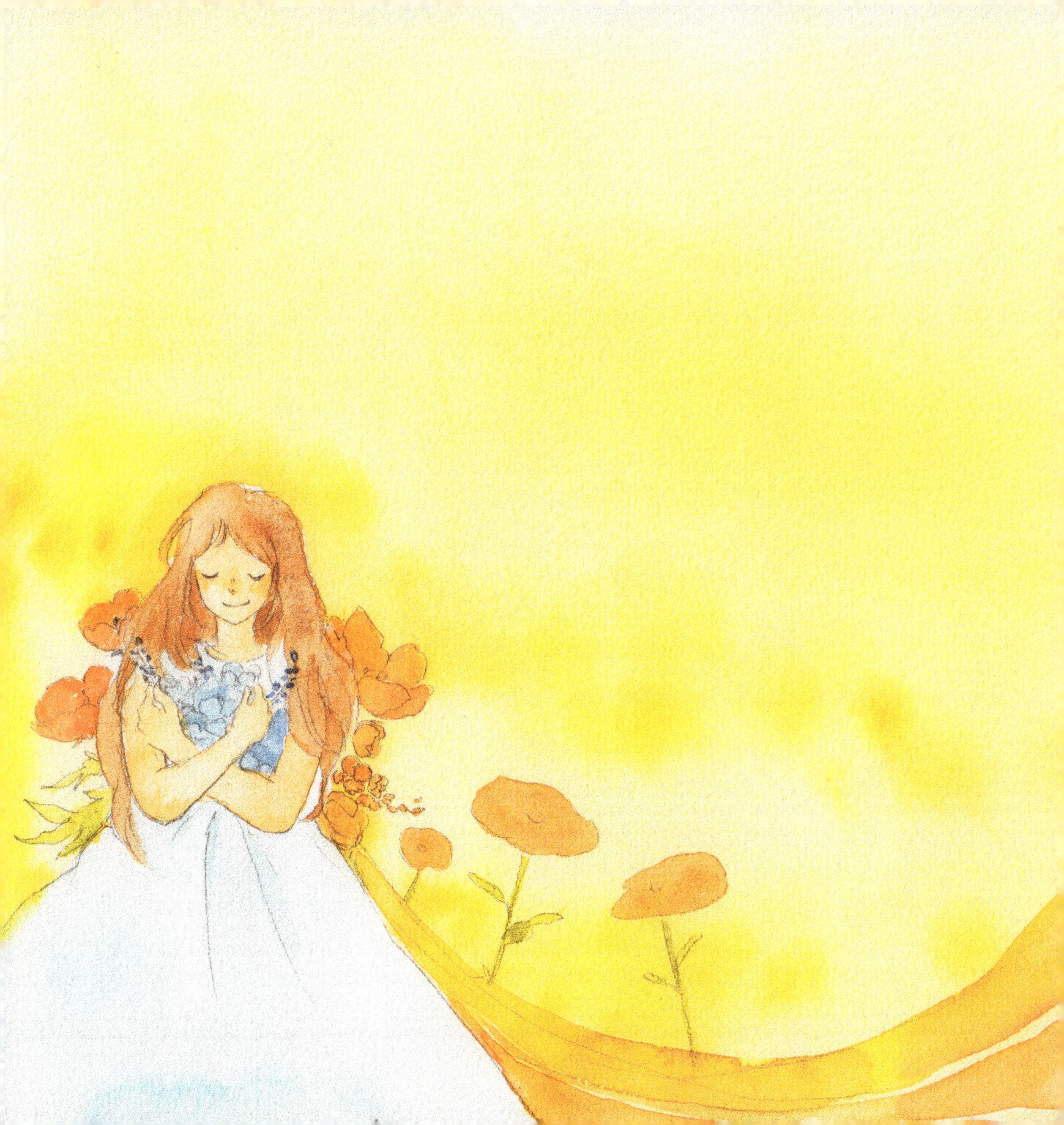

Zest is feeling excited about life as much as you can.
Seeing the sunny side rather than looking for all that is wrong.
Viewing life as a beautiful song.

While there may be some dark clouds along the way,
Always believing that tomorrow is a new day.

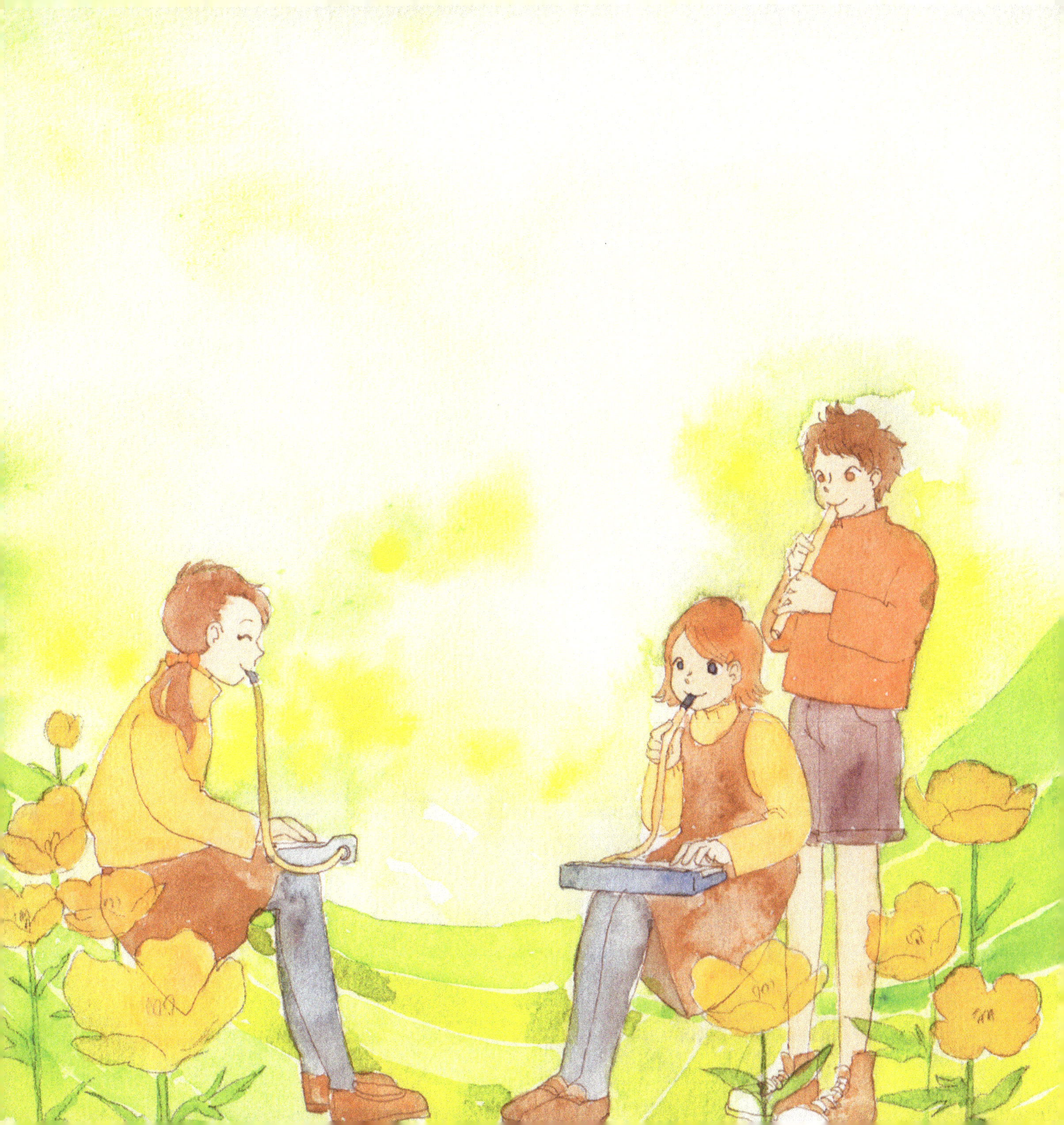

HUMANITY

Love is feeling close to people and wanting to show that you care.
Always missing them when they are not there.

Love is not focusing just on you.
Rather than one, you now think about two.

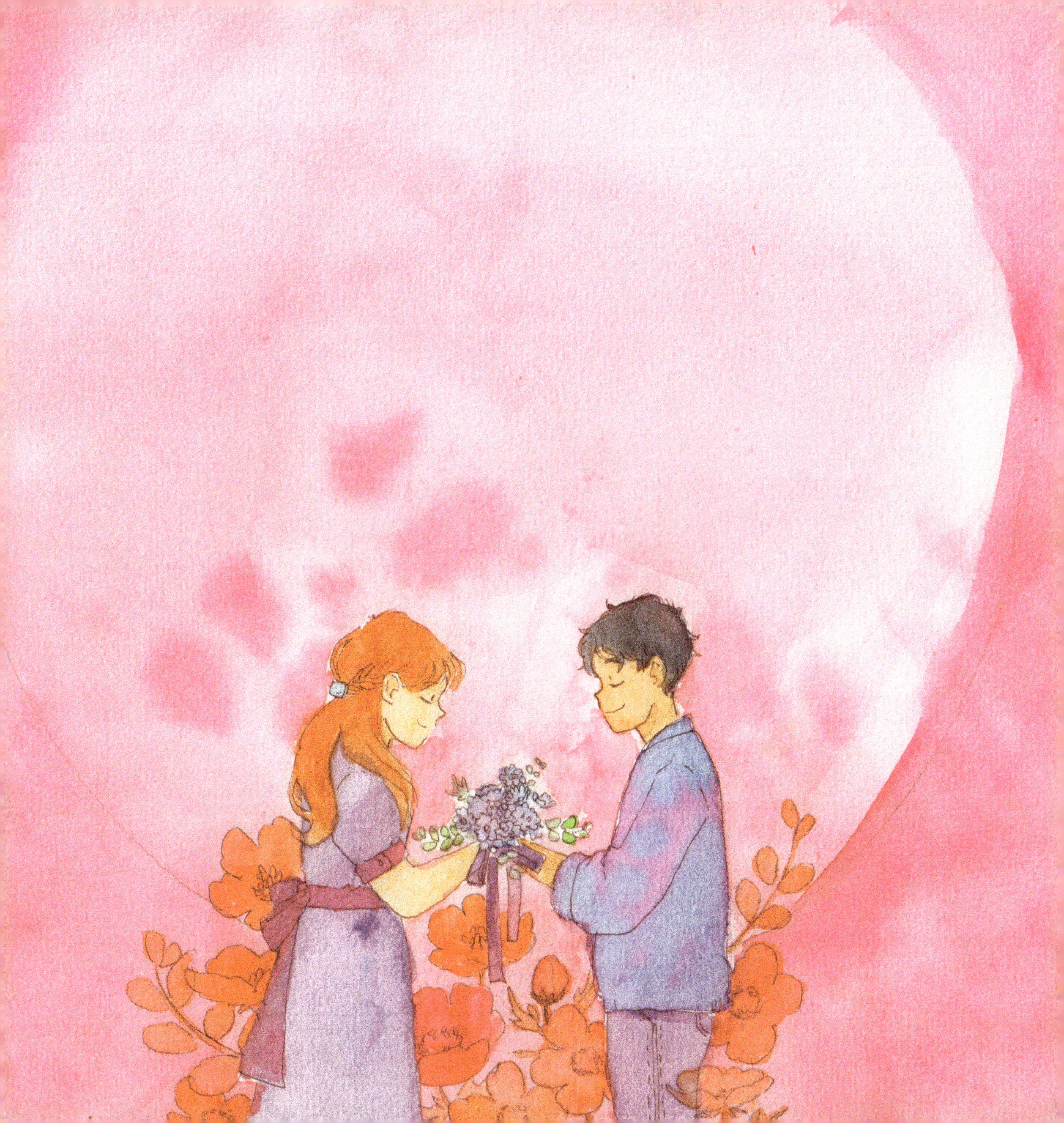

Kindness is going out of our way.
Saying good morning and have a great day.

It's holding a door for a person you don't know.
Cheering someone up when they feel low.

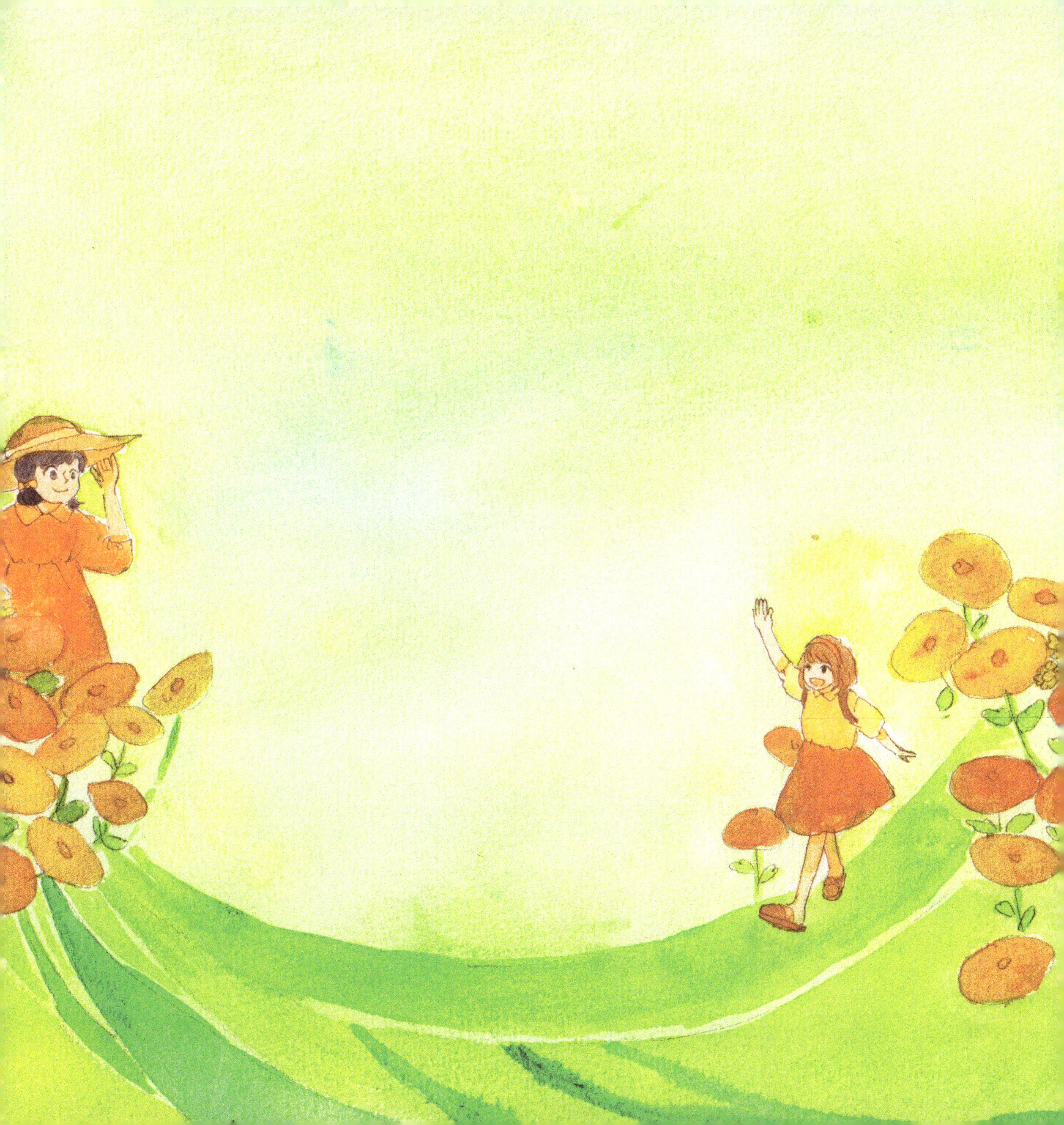

Social intelligence is being aware of what others may think and feel.
And counting these thoughts and feelings as all very real.

It's making decisions taking in another's point of view.
And not just counting the view of you.

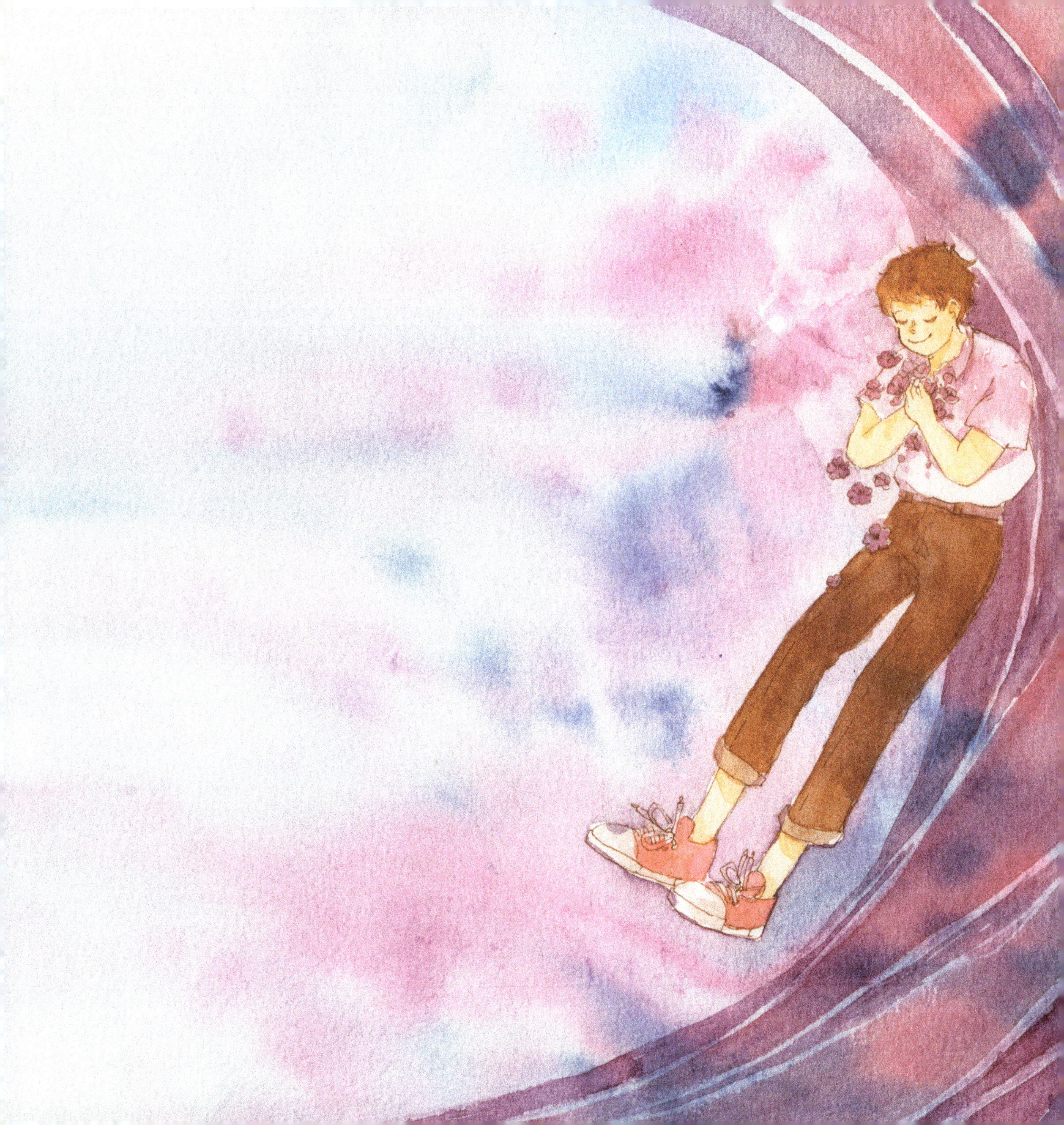

JUSTICE

Teamwork is being part of a group and doing your share.
Treating members equally because that's what's fair.

You are not the one who always has to stand out.
This is true beyond a doubt.

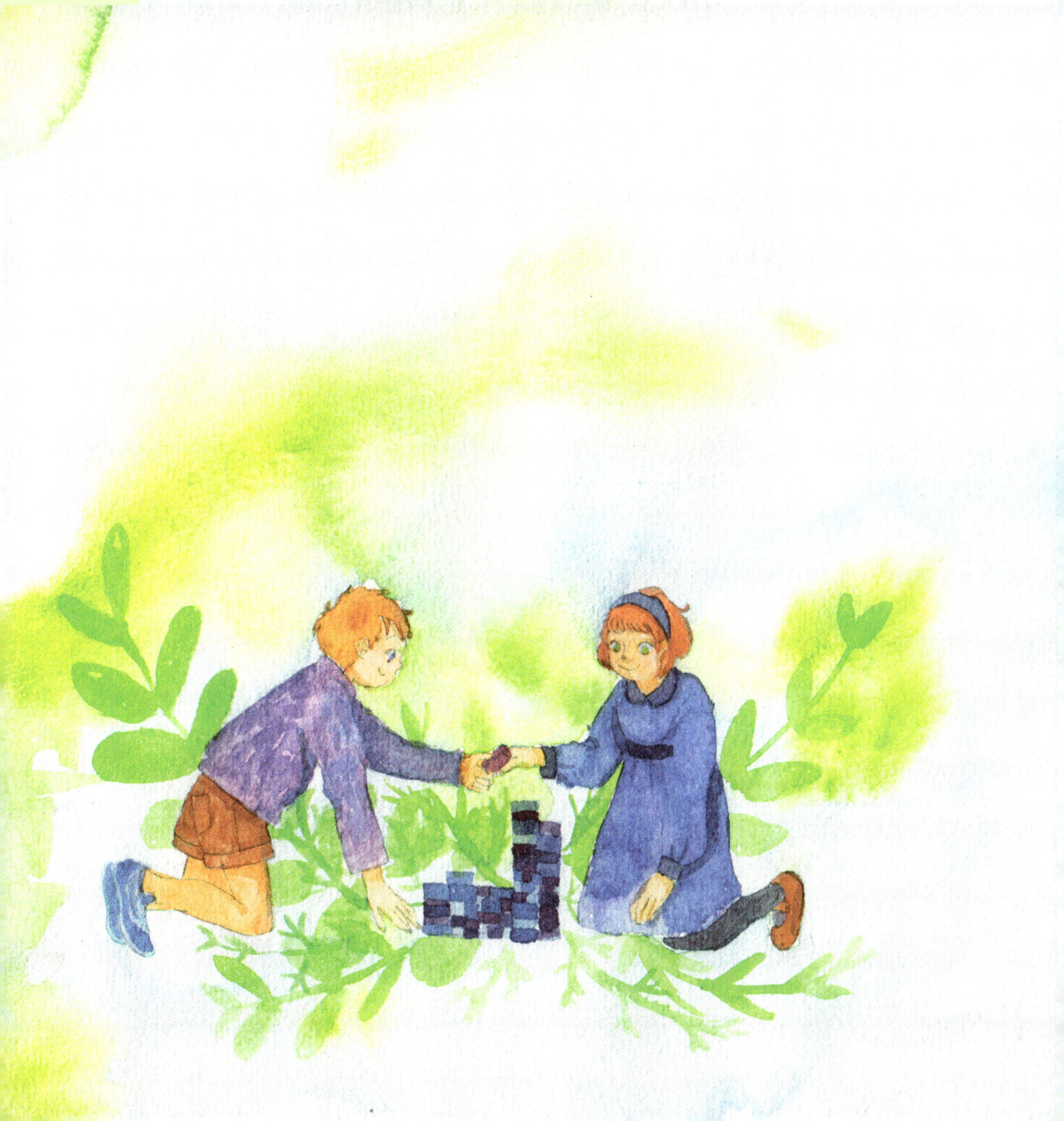

Fairness is doing what's right for everyone and not just you.
Or for that matter just a select few.

It is trying to make what's wrong right and not just let wrong be.
This is true for you as well as for me.

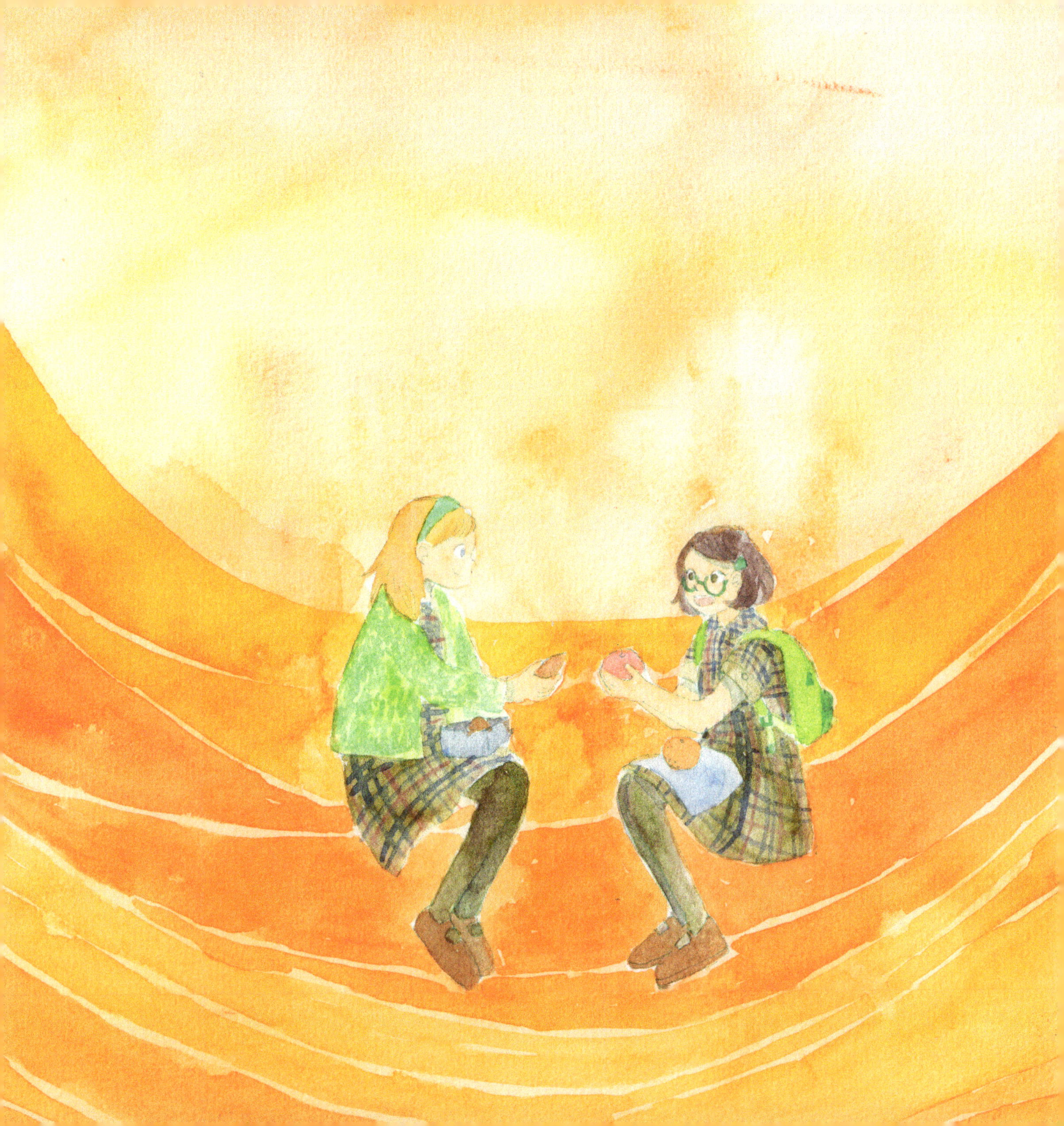

Leadership is encouraging others to get things done.
Taking charge without taking over, I would say.

Leading them toward a goal.
Helping them find their way.

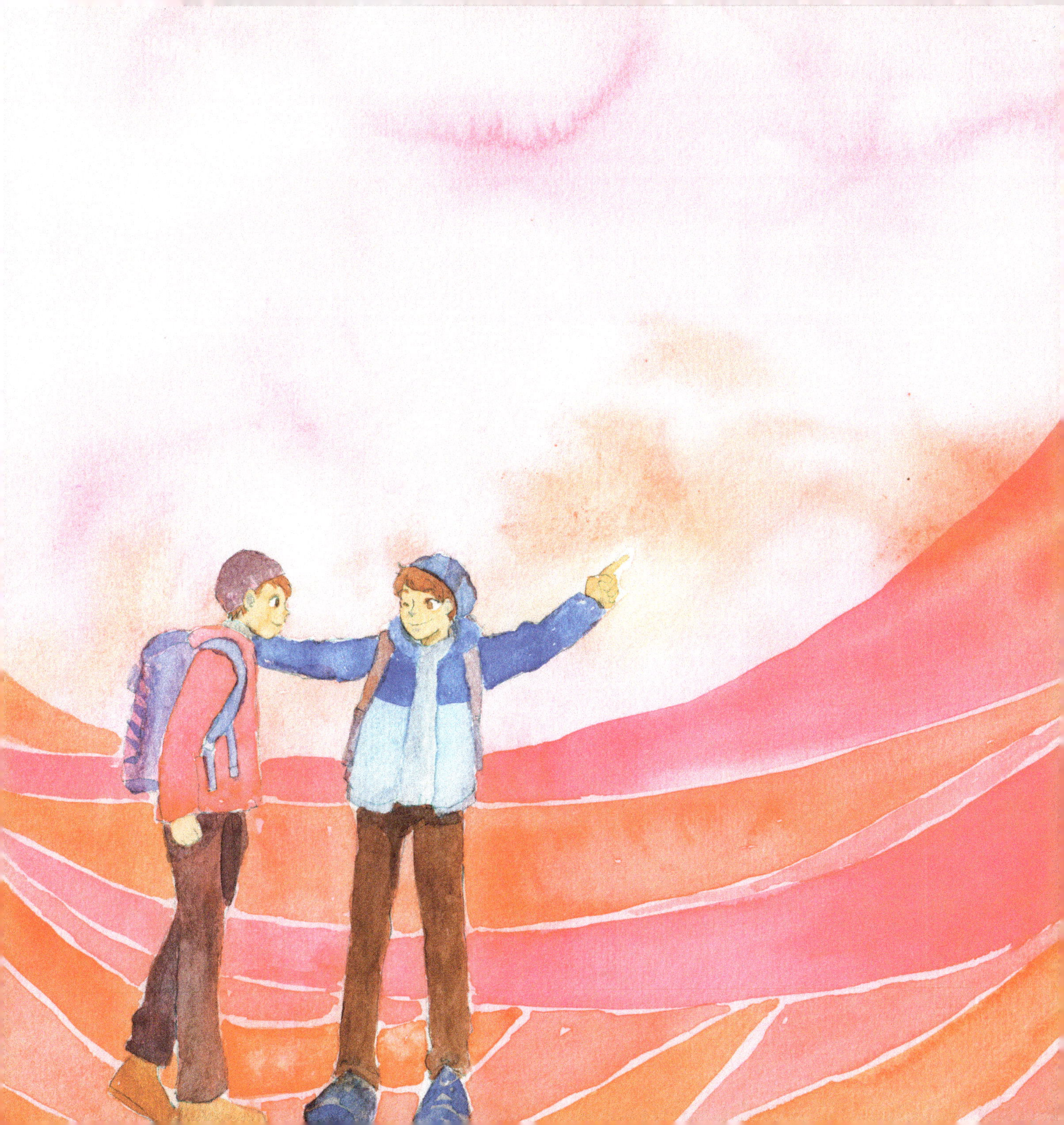

TEMPERANCE

Forgiveness is giving others a second chance
And not holding a grudge.
It is having an open mind and not one that won't budge.

Forgiveness can sometimes bring people closer than before.
With so many good times in store.

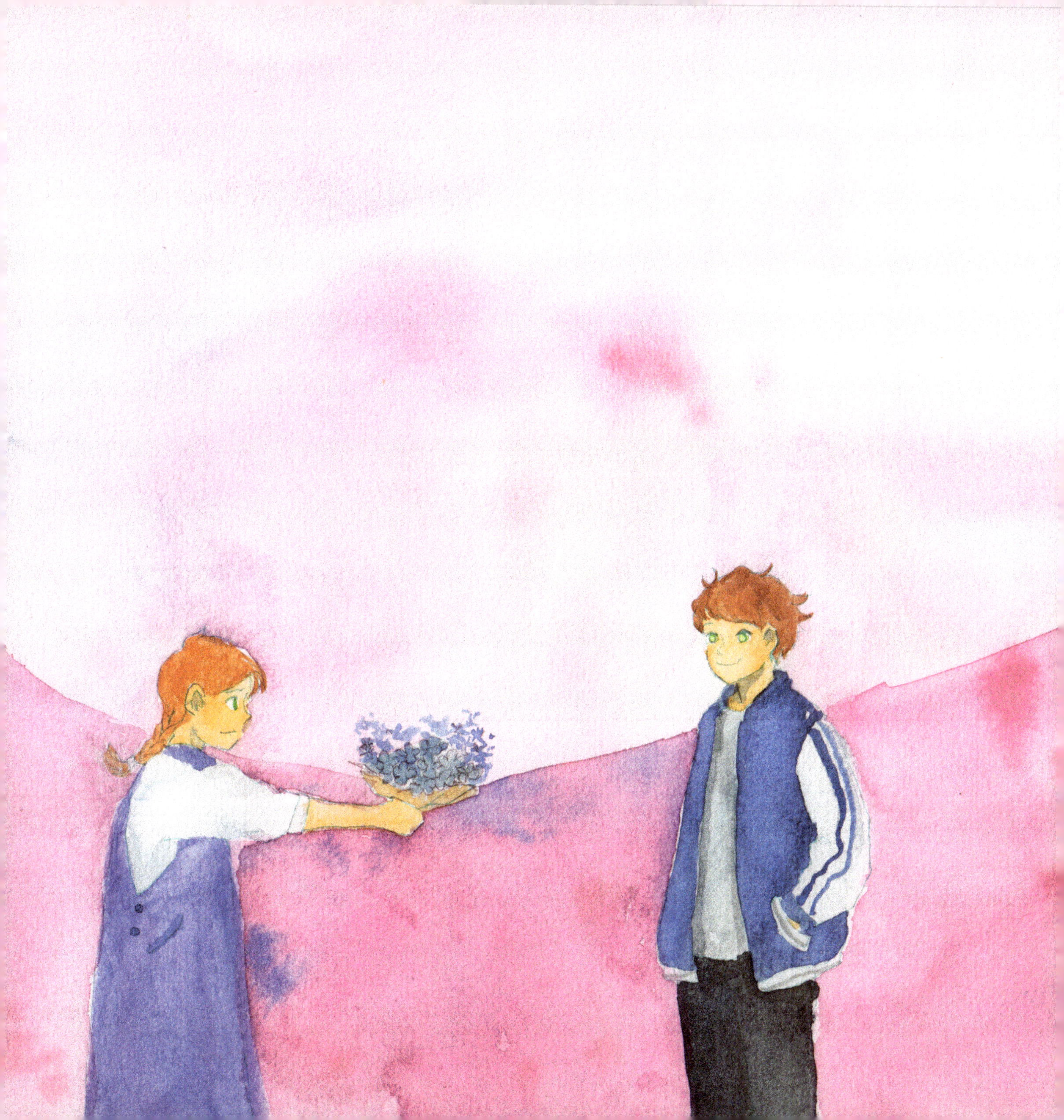

Humility is not seeing yourself as special or better
than anyone you know.
It is being who you are
And not putting on a show.

It is not bragging or boasting to make yourself feel good.
It's about being you, just as you should.

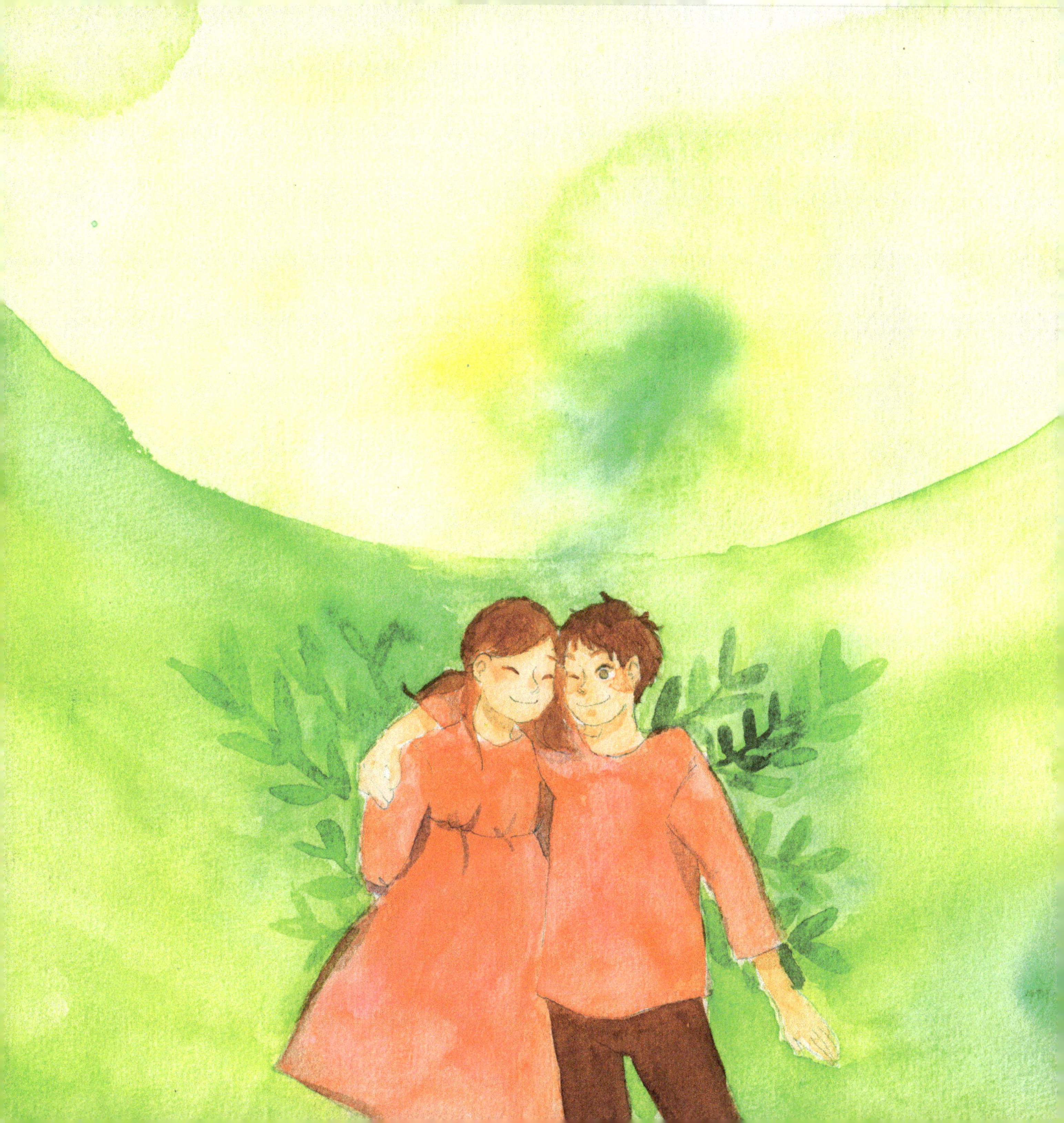

Prudence is being careful about what you do and say,
So when all is done you do not feel sorry in any way.

It's not saying things meant to hurt or tease people you know.
It is being thoughtful wherever you go.

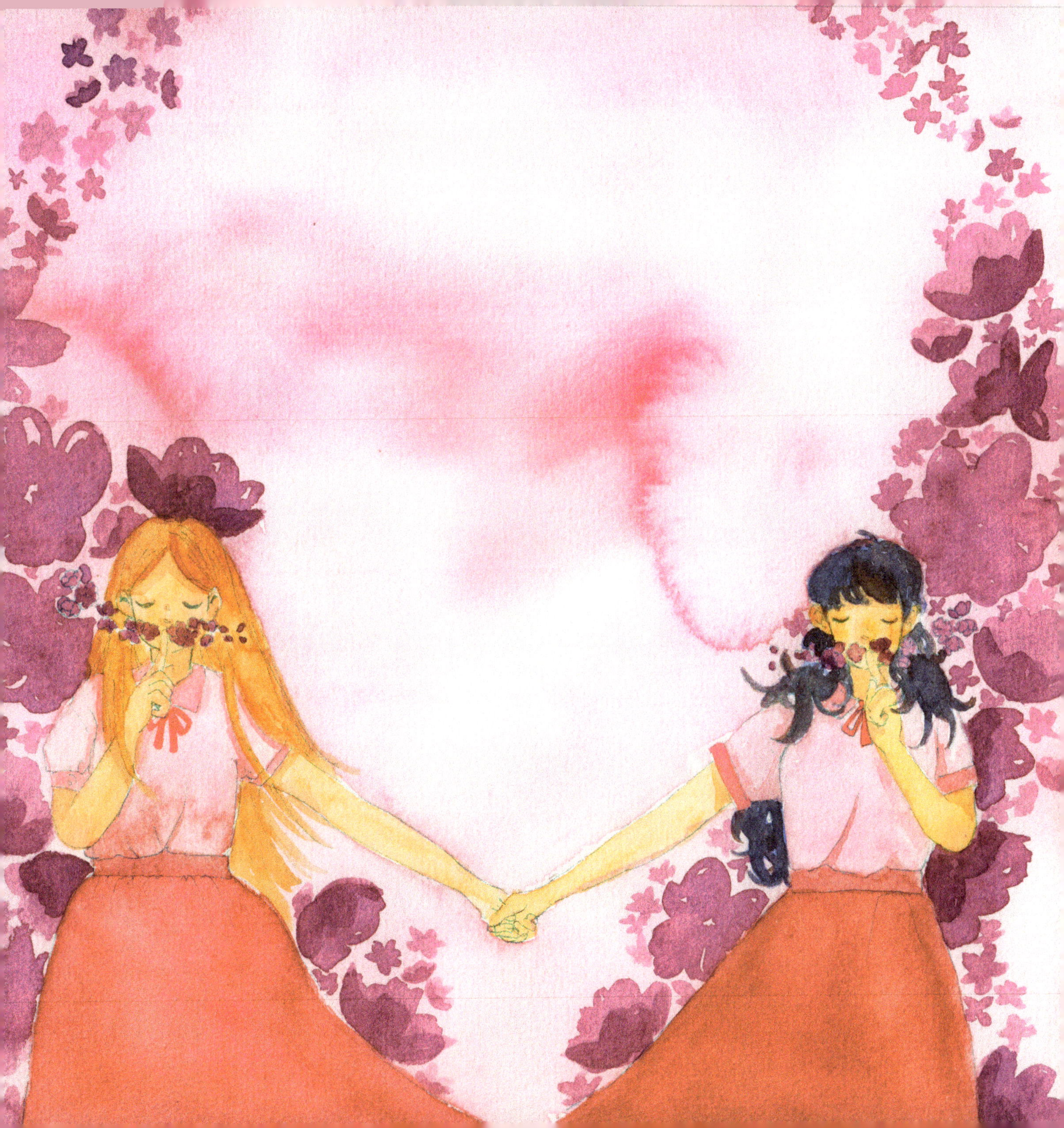

Self-regulation is controlling your actions and learning to wait
your turn as much as you can.
It's learning to take a breath and count to ten.

It's not pushing ahead of the line and blurting out what we have to say.
It is practicing self-control each and every day.

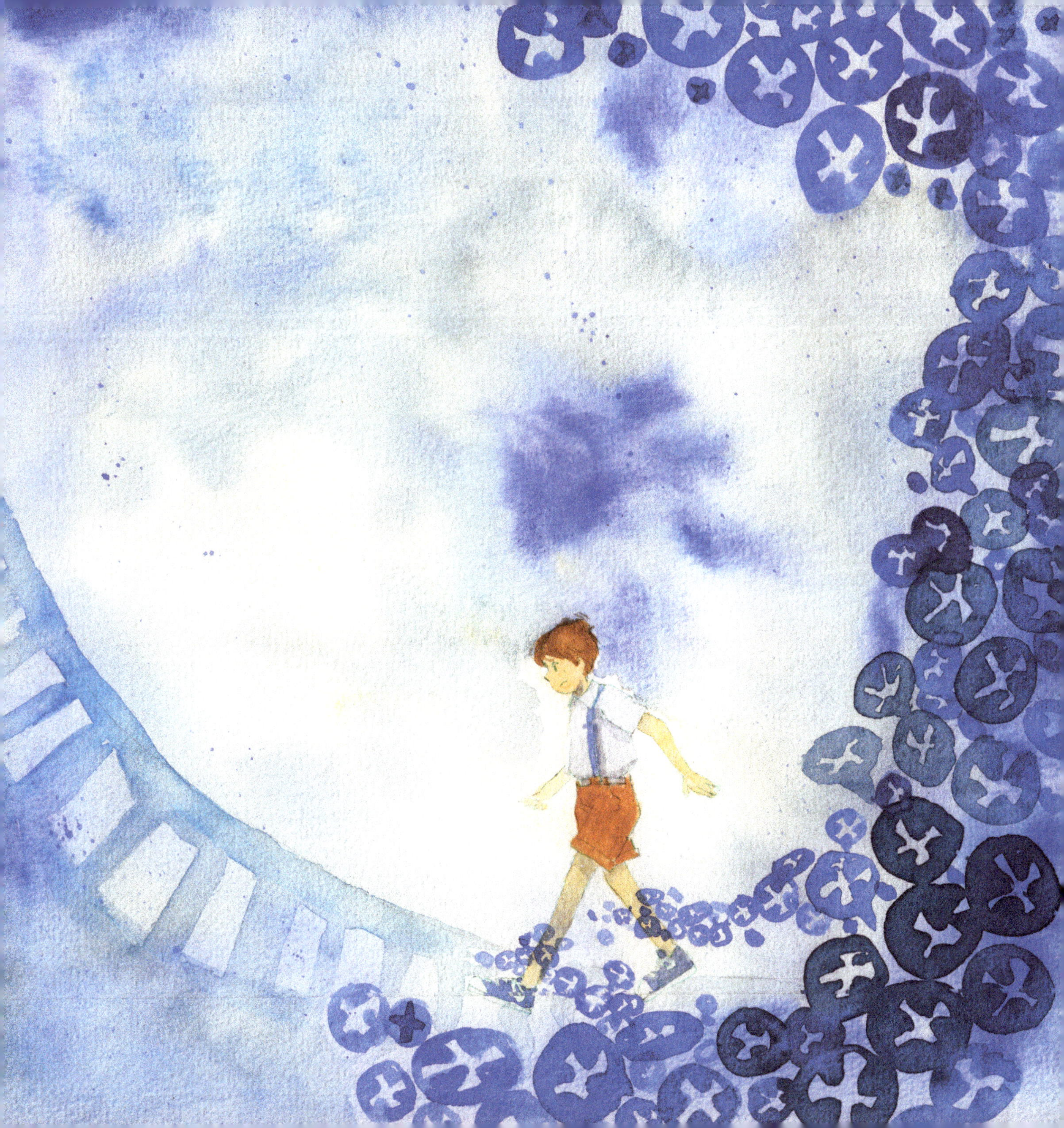

TRANSCENDENCE

Appreciation of beauty and excellence is seeing the world
with wonder and awe.
The flowers, trees, rivers, oceans, watching a bird soar.

The silvery moon, the sparkling stars, the snow-capped mountains
and much, much more.

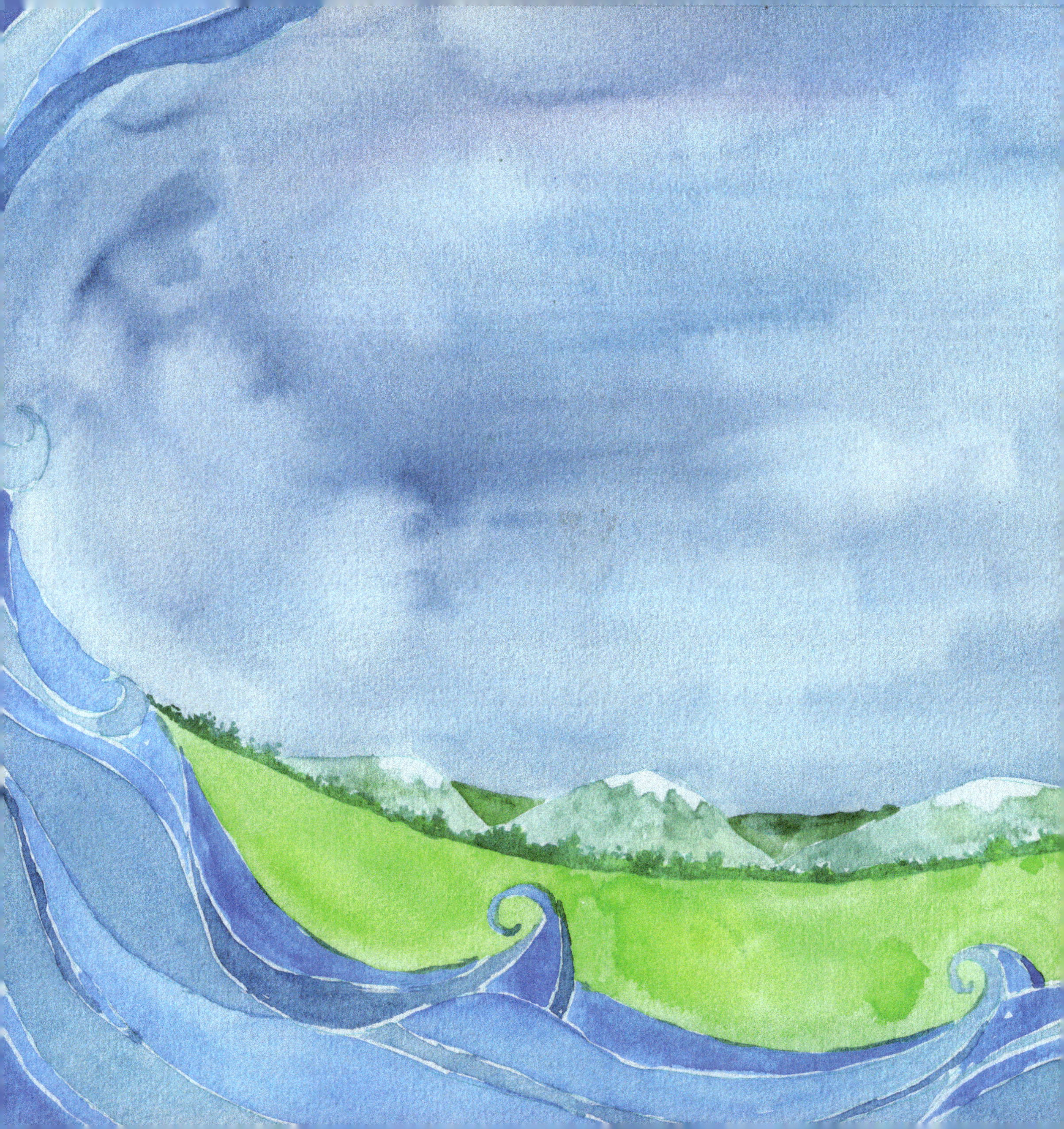

Gratitude is being thankful for what we have and who we are.
Taking time to express thanks for everything and everyone, near and far.

It is reminding ourselves of all that we have
when we think we have none.
That behind every cloud, there is a golden sun.

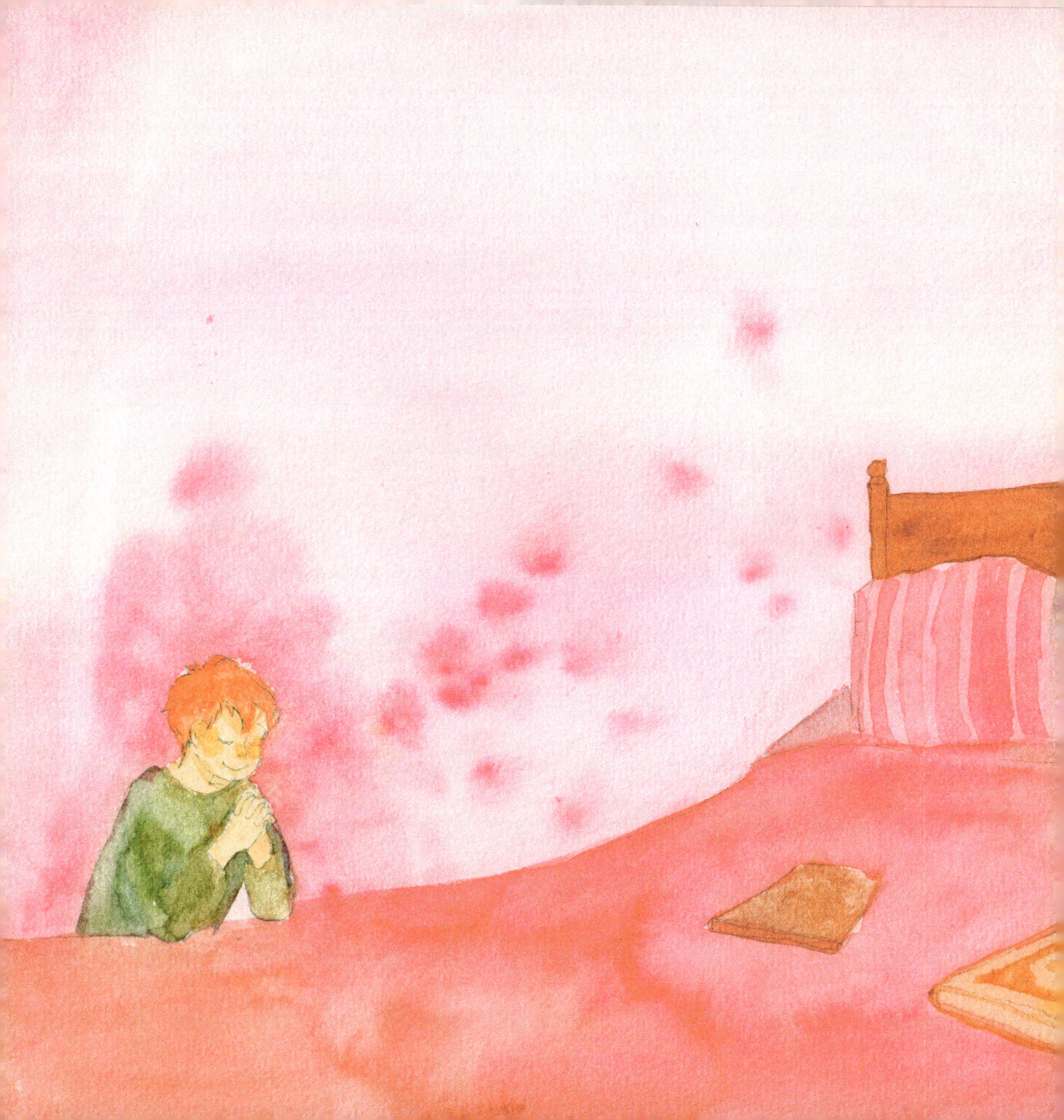

Hope is looking to a future that is bright
Where things are not dark as the black of night.

Looking to a guiding star,
Wherever we find ourselves, wherever we are.
Knowing that with hope we can travel so far.

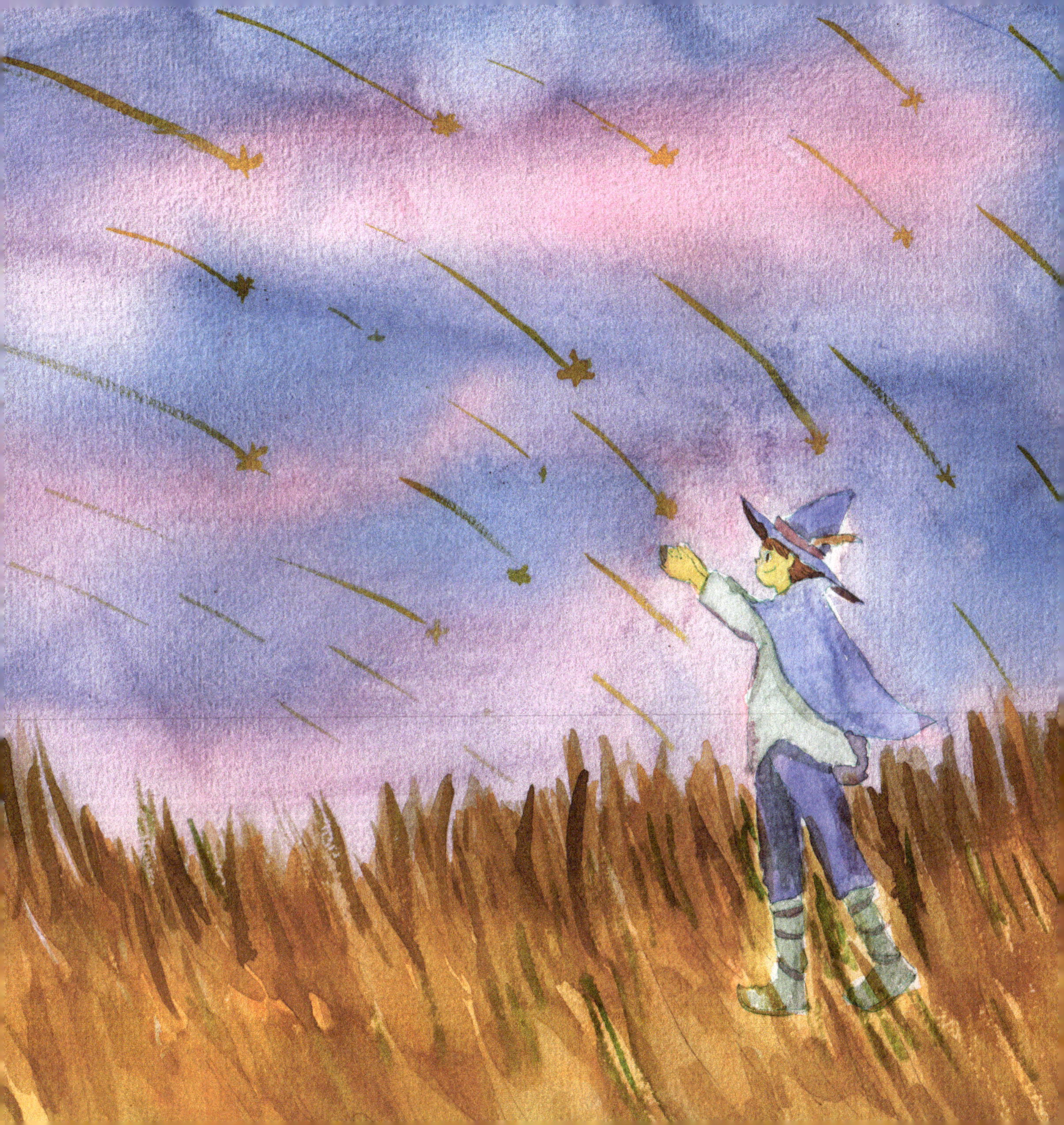

Humor is seeing the funny side of life where others may see none.
It is knowing how to laugh and to have fun.

But, is not making fun of, that's for sure.
Humor helps people not to feel less, but rather to feel more.

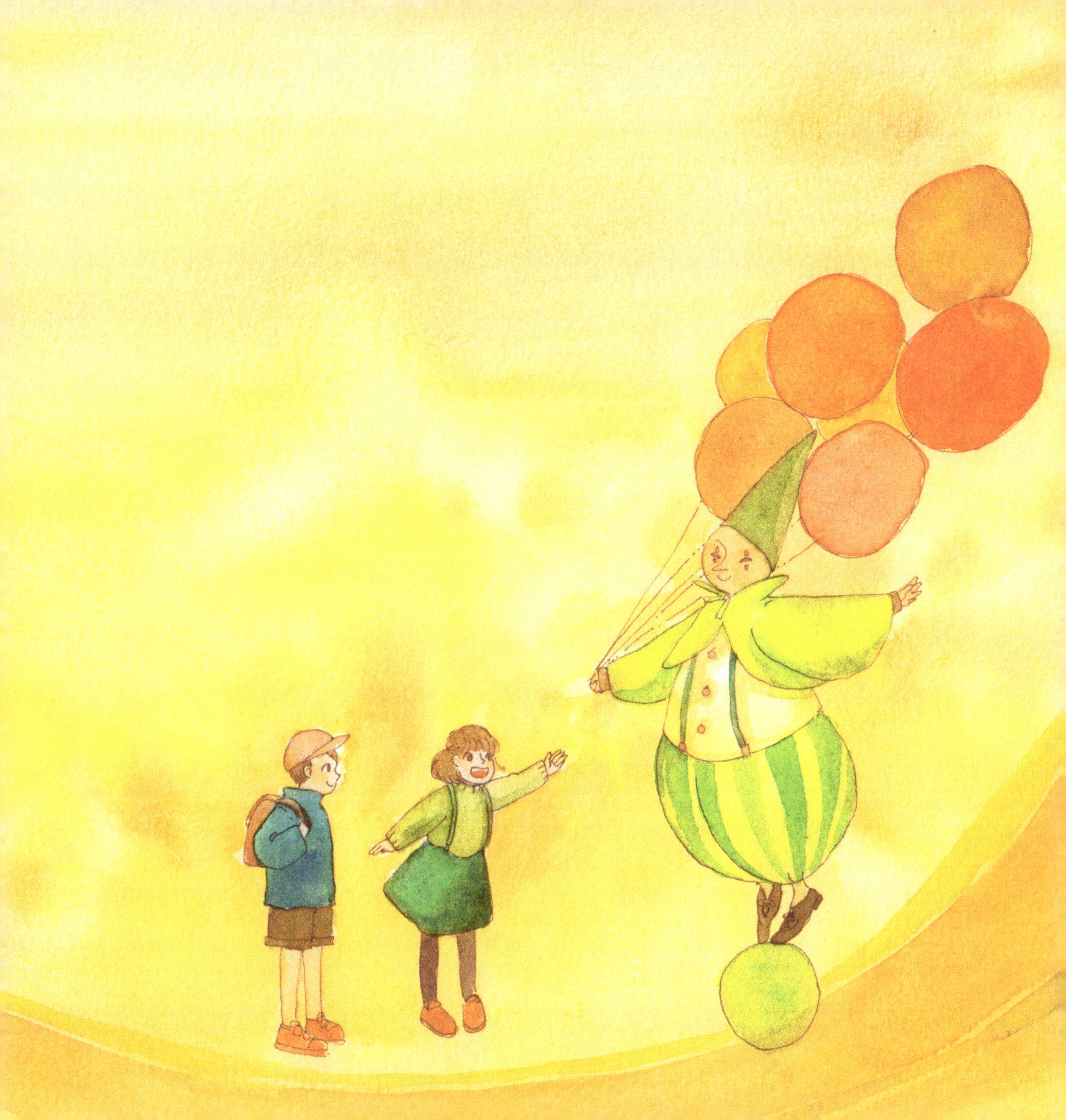

Spirituality is looking for meaning in life, things that make everything seem worthwhile.

Reading a good book, gazing up at the stars, chatting with a friend. Helping people out, writing a story, taking a hike in the woods, the possibilities never end.

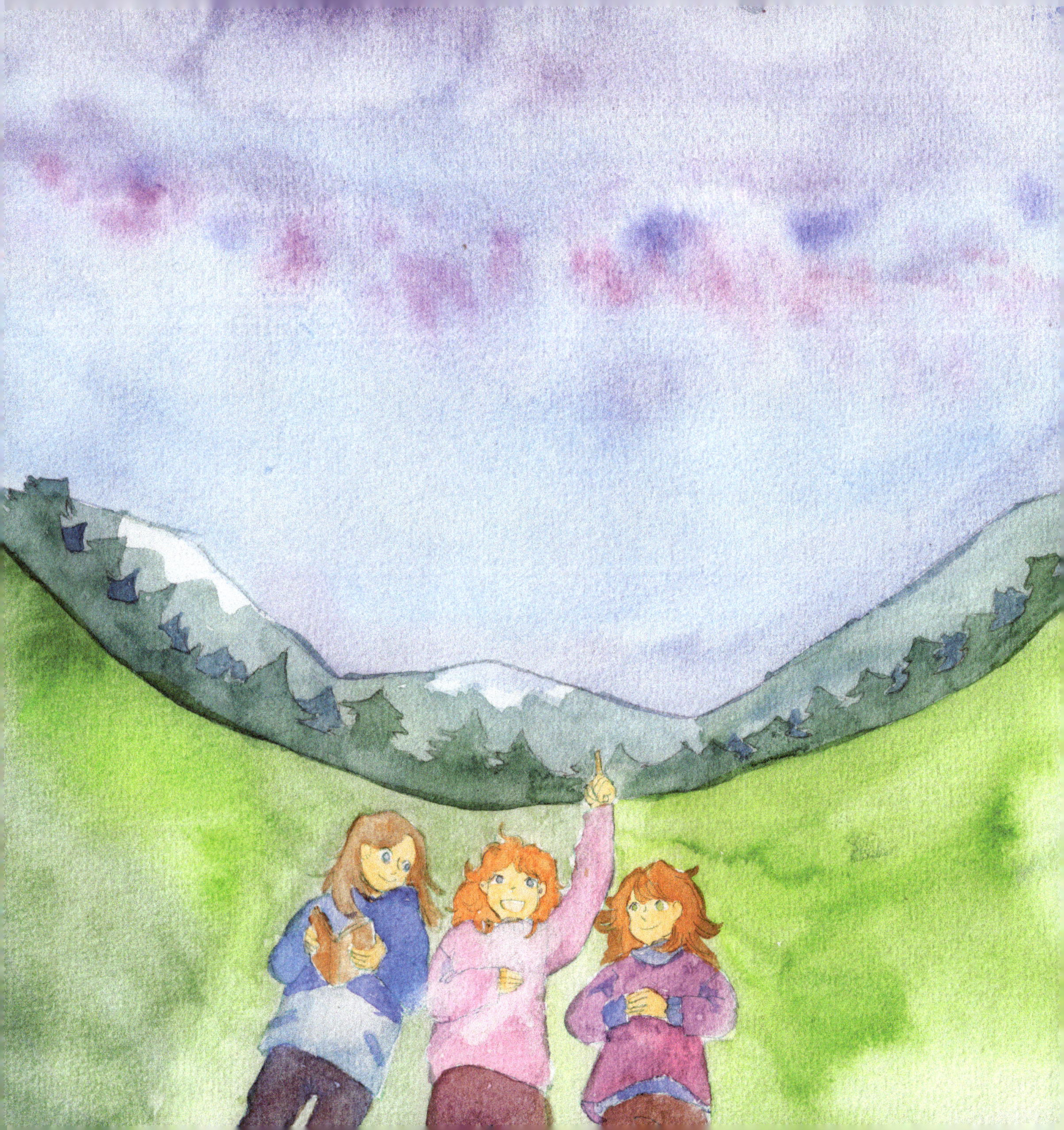

CPSIA information can be obtained
at www.ICGtesting.com
Printed in the USA
BVHW02s1028150418
513432BV00026B/729/P